United States Government Accountability Office

GAO

Testimony
Before the Committee on Oversight and
Government Reform, House of
Representatives

For Release on Delivery
Expected at 9:30 a.m. EST
Tuesday, February 28, 2012

More Efficient and Effective Government: Opportunities to Reduce Duplication, Overlap and Fragmentation, Achieve Savings, and Enhance Revenue

Statement of Gene L. Dodaro
Comptroller General of the United States

I0426056

G A O
Accountability ★ Integrity ★ Reliability

GAO-12-449T

Mr. Chairman, Ranking Member Cummings, and Members of the Committee:

Thank you for the opportunity to discuss our 2012 annual report, which presents 51 areas where programs may be able to achieve greater efficiencies or become more effective in providing government services by reducing potential duplication, overlap, or fragmentation in federal programs and activities.[1] We have also continued to monitor developments in the 81 areas that we identified a year ago in the first report we issued in this series.[2] Our 2011 follow-up report released today describes the extent to which progress has been made to address these areas.[3] Appendix I presents a summary of our assessment of the overall progress made in each area.

My testimony is based on our 2012 annual and 2011 follow-up reports. Specifically, it addresses: (1) federal programs or functional areas where unnecessary duplication, overlap, or fragmentation exists, as well as other opportunities for potential cost savings or enhanced revenues; (2) status of actions taken by Congress and the executive branch to address the areas we identified in our 2011 report; (3) aspects of the GPRA Modernization Act of 2010 that may contribute to addressing and preventing duplication, overlap and fragmentation among federal programs; and (4) our approach to identifying duplication or cost savings in federal programs and activities. We conducted our work in accordance with generally accepted government auditing standards or with our quality assurance framework, as appropriate. For issues where information is being reported on for the first time in this report, we sought comments from the agencies involved, and incorporated those comments as appropriate. In updating the actions we identified in the 2011 annual report, we asked the agencies involved and the Office of Management

---

[1]GAO, *2012 Annual Report: Opportunities to Reduce Duplication, Overlap and Fragmentation, Achieve Savings, and Enhance Revenue*, GAO-12-342SP (Washington, D.C.: Feb. 28, 2012).

[2]GAO, *Opportunities to Reduce Potential Duplication in Government Programs, Save Tax Dollars, and Enhance Revenue*, GAO-11-318SP (Washington, D.C.: Mar. 1, 2011).

[3]GAO, *Follow-up on 2011 Report: Status of Actions Taken to Reduce Duplication, Overlap, and Fragmentation, Save Tax Dollars, and Enhance Revenue*, GAO-12-453SP (Washington, D.C.: Feb. 28, 2012).

and Budget (OMB) for their review and incorporated comments as appropriate.

We identified 51 areas in our 2012 annual report, including 32 areas of potential duplication, overlap, or fragmentation as well as 19 opportunities for agencies or Congress to consider taking action that could either reduce the cost of government operations or enhance revenue collections for the Treasury. These areas involve a wide range of government missions including agriculture, defense, economic development, education, energy, general government, health, homeland security, international affairs, science and the environment, and social services. Within and across these missions, the 2012 annual report touches on virtually all major federal departments and agencies. We expanded the scope of our work for this year's report to focus on areas where a mix of federal approaches is used, such as tax expenditures, direct spending, and federal grant or loan programs.

In our 2011 follow-up report, we assessed the extent to which Congress and the executive branch addressed the 81 areas—including a total of 176 actions—to reduce or eliminate unnecessary duplication, overlap, or fragmentation or achieve other potential financial benefits. As of February 10, 2012, Congress and the executive branch have made some progress in addressing the majority of the 81 areas we identified; however, additional steps are needed to fully implement the remaining actions. Specifically, our assessment found that all actions had been addressed in 4 areas, partially addressed in 60 areas, and not addressed in 17 areas. In addition, OMB has instructed agencies to consider areas of duplication or overlap identified in our 2011 report and by others in their fiscal year 2013 budget submissions and management plans. The OMB guidance also advised agencies to take a number of other steps to enhance efficiency, such as identifying and including in their budget submissions cost-saving efforts that will improve operational efficiency and taxpayers' rate of return, including program integration, reorganizations within and between agency components, and resource realignment to improve public services.

Under requirements established by the GPRA Modernization Act of 2010 (the Act),[4] OMB is also required to coordinate with agencies to establish

---

[4]Pub. L. No. 111-352, 124 Stat. 3866 (2011), amending Pub. L. No. 103-62, 107 Stat. 285 (1993).

outcome-oriented goals covering a limited number of crosscutting policy areas as well as goals to improve management across the federal government, and develop a governmentwide performance plan for making progress toward achieving those goals. The President's budget for 2013 includes 14 such crosscutting policy goals. Aspects of several of these goals—including Science, Technology, Engineering, and Math Education, Entrepreneurship and Small Businesses, Job Training, Cybersecurity, Information Technology Management, Procurement and Acquisition Management, and Real Property Management—are discussed in our March 2011 and February 2012 reports. The Act's requirements provide a much needed basis for more fully integrating a wide array of potentially duplicative, overlapping, or fragmented federal activities as well as a cohesive perspective on the long-term goals of the federal government focused on priority policy areas.

Opportunities exist for the Congress and federal agencies to continue to address the needed actions identified in our March 2011 and February 2012 reports. Collectively, these reports show that, if the actions are implemented, the government could potentially save tens of billions of dollars annually. Cost savings related to reducing or eliminating duplication, overlap, and fragmentation can be difficult to estimate because the portion of agency budgets devoted to certain programs or activities is often unclear, or needed information on program performance or costs is not readily available. In some cases, there is sufficient information to estimate potential savings or other benefits if actions are taken to address individual issues. In other cases, estimates of cost savings or other benefits would depend upon what congressional and executive branch decisions were made, including how certain of our recommendations are implemented. Nevertheless, considering the amount of program dollars involved in the issues we have identified, even limited adjustments could result in significant savings. Additionally, we have found that agencies can often realize other kinds of benefits, such as improved customer service and decreased administrative burdens.

2012 Annual Report Identified 51 Opportunity Areas

Our 2012 annual report identified 51 areas where unnecessary duplication, overlap, or fragmentation exists as well as additional opportunities for potential cost savings or enhanced revenues. We identified about 130 specific actions that Congress or the executive branch could take to address these areas.

We identified 32 areas where government missions are fragmented across multiple agencies or programs; agencies, offices, or initiatives may have similar or overlapping objectives or may provide similar services to similar populations or target similar users; and when two or more agencies or programs are engaged in the same activities or provide the same services to the same beneficiaries (see table 1). We found instances where multiple government programs or activities have led to inefficiencies, and we determined that greater efficiencies or effectiveness might be achievable.

Table 1: Duplication, Overlap, and Fragmentation Areas Identified

Mission		Areas identified
Agriculture	1.	**Protection of Food and Agriculture**: Centrally coordinated oversight is needed to ensure nine federal agencies effectively and efficiently implement the nation's fragmented policy to defend the food and agriculture systems against potential terrorist attacks and major disasters.
Defense	2.	**Electronic Warfare**: Identifying opportunities to consolidate Department of Defense airborne electronic attack programs could reduce overlap in the department's multiple efforts to develop new capabilities and improve the department's return on its multibillion-dollar acquisition investments.
	3.	**Unmanned Aircraft Systems**: Ineffective acquisition practices and collaboration efforts in the Department of Defense unmanned aircraft systems portfolio creates overlap and the potential for duplication among a number of current programs and systems.
	4.	**Counter-Improvised Explosive Device Efforts**: The Department of Defense continues to risk duplication in its multibillion-dollar counter-improvised explosive device efforts because it does not have a comprehensive database of its projects and initiatives.
	5.	**Defense Language and Culture Training**: The Department of Defense needs a more integrated approach to reduce fragmentation in training approaches and overlap in the content of training products acquired by the military services and other organizations.
	6.	**Stabilization, Reconstruction, and Humanitarian Assistance Efforts**: Improving the Department of Defense's evaluations of stabilization, reconstruction, and humanitarian assistance efforts, and addressing coordination challenges with the Department of State and the U.S. Agency for International Development, could reduce overlapping efforts and result in the more efficient use of taxpayer dollars.
Economic development	7.	**Support for Entrepreneurs**: Overlap and fragmentation among the economic development programs that support entrepreneurial efforts require the Office of Management and Budget and other agencies to better evaluate the programs and explore opportunities for program restructuring, which may include consolidation, within and across agencies.
	8.	**Surface Freight Transportation**: Fragmented federal programs and funding structures are not maximizing the efficient movement of freight.
Energy	9.	**Department of Energy Contractor Support Costs**: The Department of Energy should assess whether further opportunities could be taken to streamline support functions, estimated to cost over $5 billion, at its contractor-managed laboratory and nuclear production and testing sites, in light of contractors' historically fragmented approach to providing these functions.
	10.	**Nuclear Nonproliferation**: Comprehensive review needed to address strategic planning limitations and potential fragmentation and overlap concerns among programs combating nuclear smuggling overseas.

Mission	Areas identified
General government	11. **Personnel Background Investigations**: The Office of Management and Budget should take action to prevent agencies from making potentially duplicative investments in electronic case management and adjudication systems.
	12. **Cybersecurity Human Capital**: Governmentwide initiatives to enhance the cybersecurity workforce in the federal government need better structure, planning, guidance, and coordination to reduce duplication.
	13. **Spectrum Management**: Enhanced coordination of federal agencies' efforts to manage radio frequency spectrum and an examination of incentive mechanisms to foster more efficient spectrum use may aid regulators' attempts to jointly respond to competing demands for spectrum while identifying valuable spectrum that could be auctioned for commercial use, thereby generating revenues for the U.S. Treasury.
Health	14. **Health Research Funding**: The National Institutes of Health, Department of Defense, and Department of Veterans Affairs can improve sharing of information to help avoid the potential for unnecessary duplication.
	15. **Military and Veterans Health Care**: The Departments of Defense and Veterans Affairs need to improve integration across care coordination and case management programs to reduce duplication and better assist servicemembers, veterans, and their families.
Homeland security/Law enforcement	16. **Department of Justice Grants**: The Department of Justice could improve how it targets nearly $3.9 billion to reduce the risk of potential unnecessary duplication across the more than 11,000 grant awards it makes annually.
	17. **Homeland Security Grants**: The Department of Homeland Security needs better project information and coordination among four overlapping grant programs.
	18. **Federal Facility Risk Assessments**: Agencies are making duplicate payments for facility risk assessments by completing their own assessments, while also paying the Department of Homeland Security for assessments that the department is not performing.
Information technology	19. **Information Technology Investment Management**: The Office of Management and Budget and the Departments of Defense and Energy need to address potentially duplicative information technology investments to avoid investing in unnecessary systems.
International affairs	20. **Overseas Administrative Services**: U.S. government agencies could lower the administrative cost of their operations overseas by increasing participation in the International Cooperative Administrative Support Services system and by reducing reliance on American officials overseas to provide these services.
	21. **Training to Identify Fraudulent Travel Documents**: Establishing a formal coordination mechanism could help reduce duplicative activities among seven different entities that are involved in training foreign officials to identify fraudulent travel documents.
Science and the environment	22. **Coordination of Space System Organizations**: Fragmented leadership has led to program challenges and potential duplication in developing multibillion-dollar space systems.
	23. **Space Launch Contract Costs**: Increased collaboration between the Department of Defense and the National Aeronautics and Space Administration could reduce launch contracting duplication.
	24. **Diesel Emissions**: Fourteen grant and loan programs at the Department of Energy, Department of Transportation, and the Environmental Protection Agency, and three tax expenditures fund activities that have the effect of reducing mobile source diesel emissions; enhanced collaboration and performance measurement could improve these fragmented and overlapping programs.
	25. **Environmental Laboratories**: The Environmental Protection Agency needs to revise its overall approach to managing its 37 laboratories to address potential overlap and fragmentation and more fully leverage its limited resources.

Mission	Areas identified
	26. **Green Building**: To evaluate the potential for overlap or fragmentation among federal green building initiatives, the Department of Housing and Urban Development, the Department of Energy, and the Environmental Protection Agency should lead other federal agencies in collaborating on assessing their investments in more than 90 initiatives to foster green building in the nonfederal sector.
Social services	27. **Social Security Benefit Coordination**: Benefit offsets for related programs help reduce the potential for overlapping payments but pose administrative challenges.
	28. **Housing Assistance**: Examining the benefits and costs of housing programs and tax expenditures that address the same or similar populations or areas, and potentially consolidating them, could help mitigate overlap and fragmentation and decrease costs.
Training, employment, and education	29. **Early Learning and Child Care**: The Departments of Education and Health and Human Services should extend their coordination efforts to other federal agencies with early learning and child care programs to mitigate the effects of program fragmentation, simplify children's access to these services, collect the data necessary to coordinate operation of these programs, and identify and minimize any unwarranted overlap and potential duplication.
	30. **Employment for People with Disabilities**: Better coordination among 50 programs in nine federal agencies that support employment for people with disabilities could help mitigate program fragmentation and overlap, and reduce the potential for duplication or other inefficiencies.
	31. **Science, Technology, Engineering, and Mathematics Education**: Strategic planning is needed to better manage overlapping programs across multiple agencies.
	32. **Financial Literacy**: Overlap among financial literacy activities makes coordination and clarification of roles and responsibilities essential, and suggests potential benefits of consolidation.

Source: GAO-12-342SP.

Overlap and fragmentation among government programs or activities can be harbingers of unnecessary duplication. In many cases, the existence of unnecessary duplication, overlap, or fragmentation can be difficult to determine with precision due to a lack of data on programs and activities. Where information has not been available that would provide conclusive evidence of duplication, overlap, or fragmentation, we often refer to "potential duplication" and, where appropriate, we suggest actions that agencies or Congress could take to either reduce that potential or to make programmatic data more reliable or transparent. In some instances of duplication, overlap, or fragmentation, it may be appropriate for multiple agencies or entities to be involved in the same programmatic or policy area due to the nature or magnitude of the federal effort.

Among the 32 areas highlighted in our 2012 annual report are the following examples of opportunities for agencies or Congress to consider taking action to reduce unnecessary duplication, overlap, or fragmentation.

- *Unmanned Aircraft Systems*: The Department of Defense (DOD) estimates that the cost of current Unmanned Aircraft Systems (UAS) acquisition programs and related systems will exceed $37.5 billion in fiscal years 2012 through 2016. The elements of DOD's planned UAS portfolio include unmanned aircraft, payloads (subsystems and equipment on a UAS configured to accomplish specific missions), and ground control stations (equipment used to handle multiple mission aspects such as system command and control). We have found that ineffective acquisition practices and collaboration efforts in DOD's UAS portfolio creates overlap and the potential for duplication among a number of current programs and systems. We have also highlighted the need for DOD to consider commonality in UAS—using the same or interchangeable subsystems and components in more than one subsystem to improve interoperability of systems—to reduce the likelihood of redundancies in UAS capabilities.

Military service-driven requirements—rather than an effective departmentwide strategy—have led to overlap in DOD's UAS capabilities, resulting in many programs and systems being pursued that have similar flight characteristics and mission requirements. Illustrative of the overlap, the Department of the Navy (Navy) plans to spend more than $3 billion to develop the Broad Area Maritime Surveillance UAS, rather than the already fielded Air Force Global Hawk system on which it was based. According to the Navy, its unique requirements necessitate modifications to the Global Hawk airframe, payload interfaces, and ground control station. However, the Navy program office was not able to provide quantitative analysis to justify the variant. According to program officials, no analysis was conducted to determine the cost effectiveness of developing the Broad Area Maritime Surveillance UAS to meet the Navy's requirements versus buying more Global Hawks.

The potential for overlap also exists among UAS subsystems and components, such as sensor payloads and ground control stations. DOD expects to spend about $9 billion to buy 42 UAS sensor payloads through fiscal year 2016. While the fact that some multiservice payloads are being developed shows the potential for collaboration, the service-centric requirements process still creates the potential for overlap, including 29 sensors in our review. Further, we identified overlap and potential duplication among 10 of 13 ground control stations that DOD plans to acquire at a cost of about $3 billion through fiscal year 2016. According to a cognizant DOD official, the associated software is about 90 percent duplicative because similar software is developed for each ground control station. DOD has created a UAS control segment working group, which is chartered to increase interoperability and enable software re-use and open systems. This could allow for greater efficiency, less redundancy, and lower costs, while potentially reducing levels of contractor proprietary data that cannot be shared across UAS programs. However, existing ground control stations already have their own architecture and migration to a new service-oriented architecture will not happen until at least 2015, almost 6 years after it began.

DOD plans to significantly expand the UAS portfolio through 2040, including five new systems in the planning stages that are expected to become formal programs in the near future. While DOD has acknowledged that many UAS systems were acquired inefficiently and has begun to take steps to improve outcomes as it expands these capabilities over the next several years, the department faces challenges in its ability to improve efficiency and reduce the potential for overlap and duplication as it buys UAS capabilities. For example, the Army and Navy are planning to spend approximately $1.6 billion to acquire separate systems that are likely to have similar capabilities to meet upcoming cargo and surveillance requirements. DOD officials state that current requirements do not preclude a joint program to meet these needs, but the Army and Navy have not yet determined whether such an approach will be used.

To reduce the likelihood of overlap and potential duplication in its UAS portfolio, we have made several prior recommendations to DOD which have not been fully implemented. While DOD generally agreed with our recommendations, the overlap in current UAS programs, as well as the continued potential in future programs, shows that DOD must still do more to implement them. In particular, we have recommended that DOD (1) re-evaluate whether a single entity would be better positioned to integrate all crosscutting efforts to improve the management and operation of UAS; (2) consider an objective, independent examination of current UAS portfolio requirements and the methods for acquiring future unmanned aircraft; and (3) direct the military services to identify specific areas where commonality can be achieved. We believe the potential for savings is significant and with DOD's renewed commitment to UAS for meeting new strategic requirements, all the more imperative.

- *Housing assistance*: In fiscal year 2010, the federal government incurred about $170 billion in obligations for housing-related programs and estimated revenue forgone for tax expenditures of which tax expenditures represent $132 billion (about 78 percent). Support for homeownership in the current economic climate has expanded dramatically with nearly all mortgage originations having direct or indirect federal assistance. The

Department of the Treasury (Treasury) and the Board of Governors of the Federal Reserve System together invested more than $1.67 trillion in Fannie Mae and Freddie Mac, the government-sponsored enterprises, which issue and guarantee mortgage-backed securities. Examining the benefits and costs of housing programs and tax expenditures that address the same or similar populations or areas, and potentially consolidating them, could help mitigate overlap and fragmentation and decrease costs.

We identified 20 different entities that administer 160 programs, tax expenditures, and other tools that supported homeownership and rental housing in fiscal year 2010. In addition, we identified 39 programs, tax expenditures, and other tools that provide assistance for buying, selling, or financing a home and eight programs and tax expenditures that provide assistance to rental property owners. We found overlap in products offered and markets served by the Department of Agriculture's (USDA) Rural Housing Service (RHS) and the Department of Housing and Urban Development's (HUD) Federal Housing Administration (FHA), among others. In September 2000 and again as part of our ongoing work, we questioned the need for maintaining separate programs for rural areas. In September 2000, we recommended that Congress consider requiring USDA and HUD to examine the benefits and costs of merging programs, such as USDA's and HUD's single-family guaranteed loan and multifamily portfolio management programs.[5]

While USDA and HUD have raised concerns about merging programs, our recent work has shown increased evidence of overlap and that some RHS and FHA programs can be consolidated. For example, the two agencies overlap in products offered (mortgage credit and rental assistance), functions performed (portfolio management and preservation), and geographic areas served. Specifically, RHS and HUD guarantee single-family and multifamily loans, as well as offer rental subsidies using similar income eligibility criteria. And, both agencies have been working to maintain and preserve existing multifamily portfolios. Although RHS may offer its products only in rural areas, it is not always the insurer of choice in those areas. For example, in fiscal year 2009 FHA insured over eight times as many single-family loans in economically distressed rural counties as RHS guaranteed. And, many RHS loan

---

[5]GAO, *Rural Housing: Options for Optimizing the Federal Role in Rural Housing Development*, GAO/RCED-00-241 (Washington, D.C.: Sept. 15, 2000).

guarantees financed properties near urban areas—56 percent of single-family guarantees made in fiscal year 2009 were in metropolitan counties.

Regarding consolidation, we found that RHS relies on more in-house staff to oversee its single-family and multifamily loan portfolio of about $93 billion than HUD relies on to manage its single-family and multifamily loan portfolio of more than $1 trillion, largely because of differences in how the programs are administered. RHS has a decentralized structure of about 500 field offices that was set up to interact directly with borrowers. RHS relies on over 1,600 full-time equivalent staff to process and service its direct single-family loans and grants. While RHS limits its direct loans to low income households and its guaranteed loans to moderate income households, FHA has no income limits and does not offer a comparable direct loan program. HUD operates about 80 field offices and primarily interacts through lenders, nonprofits, and other intermediaries. RHS and FHA programs both utilize FHA-approved lenders and underwriting processes based on FHA's scorecard—an automated tool that evaluates new mortgage loans. RHS has about 530 full-time equivalent staff to process its single-family guaranteed loans. FHA relies on lenders to process its loans. Although FHA insures far more mortgages than RHS guarantees, FHA has just over 1,000 full-time equivalent staff to oversee lenders and appraisers and contractors that manage foreclosed properties. While the number of RHS field offices decreased by about 40 percent since 2000, its decentralized field structure continues to reflect the era in which it was established—the 1930s, when geography and technology greatly limited communication and transportation. These limitations have diminished and HUD programs can be used in all areas of the country.

We first recommended in September 2000 —and have followed up since then—that Congress consider requiring USDA and HUD to examine the benefits and costs of merging those programs that serve similar markets and provide similar products, and require these same agencies to explore merging their single family insured lending and multifamily portfolio management programs. At that time, USDA stated that some of the suggestions made in our report to improve the effectiveness of current programs may better serve rural areas. However, USDA also stated that the gap in housing affordability between rural and urban areas, as well as the importance of rural housing programs to the Department's broader Rural Development mission area, would make merging RHS's programs with HUD's programs unfeasible and detrimental to rural America. HUD also stated that it believes any opportunity to improve the delivery of rural housing services should be explored, but stated that the differences between RHS's and FHA's single-family programs are sizable and that without legislative changes to product terms, efforts to merge the programs would likely result in a more cumbersome rather than a more efficient delivery system. HUD added that it had been working with USDA in a mutual exchange of information on best practices and would explore possible avenues of coordination.

The agencies have been working to align certain requirements of the various multifamily housing programs. In addition, in February 2011, the Administration reported to Congress that it would establish a task force to evaluate the potential for coordinating or consolidating the housing loan programs of HUD, USDA, and the Department of Veterans Affairs (VA). According to HUD, a benchmarking effort associated with the task force was recently begun. Our ongoing work considers options for consolidating these programs and we expect to make additional related recommendations.

Furthermore, Treasury and the Internal Revenue Service (IRS) provide numerous types of housing assistance through tax expenditures. Although often necessary to meet federal priorities, some tax expenditures can contribute to mission fragmentation and program overlap that, in turn, can create service gaps, additional costs, and the potential for duplication. For example, to qualify for a historic preservation tax credit, rehabilitation must preserve historic character, which may conflict with states' efforts to produce energy-efficient, low-income properties with tax credits, and could increase project costs.

We recommended in September 2005 and reiterated in March 2011 that coordinated reviews of tax expenditures with related spending programs could help policymakers reduce overlap and inconsistencies and direct scarce resources to the most-effective or least-costly methods to deliver federal support.[6] Specifically, we recommended that the Director of OMB, in consultation with the Secretary of the Treasury, develop and implement a framework for conducting performance reviews of tax expenditures. OMB, citing methodological and conceptual issues, disagreed with our 2005 recommendations. To date, OMB had not used its budget and performance review processes to systematically review tax expenditures

---

[6]See GAO, *Government Performance and Accountability: Tax Expenditures Represent a Substantial Federal Commitment and Need to Be Reexamined*, GAO-05-690 (Washington, D.C.: Sept. 23, 2005) and GAO-11-318SP.

and promote integrated reviews of related tax and spending programs. However, in its fiscal year 2012 budget guidance, OMB instructed agencies, where appropriate, to analyze how to better integrate tax and spending policies with similar objectives and goals. The GPRA Modernization Act of 2010 also envisions such an approach for selected cross-cutting areas. Such an analysis could help identify redundancies.

- *Military and veterans health care*: We found that DOD and VA need to improve integration across care coordination and case management programs to reduce duplication and better assist servicemembers, veterans, and their families. DOD and VA have care coordination[7] and case management[8] programs that are intended to provide continuity of care for wounded, ill, and injured servicemembers and veterans. DOD and VA established the Wounded, Ill, and Injured Senior Oversight Committee (Senior Oversight Committee) to address identified problems in providing care to wounded, ill, and injured servicemembers as well as veterans. Under the purview of this committee, the departments developed the Federal Recovery Coordination Program (FRCP), a joint program administered by VA that was designed to coordinate clinical and nonclinical services for "severely" wounded, ill, and injured servicemembers—who are most likely to be medically separated from the military—across DOD, VA, other federal agencies, states, and the private sector. Separately, the Recovery Coordination Program (RCP) was established in response to the National Defense Authorization Act for Fiscal Year 2008 to improve the care, management, and transition of recovering servicemembers. It is a DOD-specific program that was designed to provide nonclinical care coordination to "seriously" wounded, ill, and injured servicemembers, who may return to active duty unlike those categorized as "severely" wounded, ill, or injured. The RCP is implemented separately by each of the military services, most of which

---

[7]According to the National Coalition on Care Coordination, care coordination is a client-centered, assessment-based interdisciplinary approach to integrating health care and social support services in which an individual's needs and preferences are assessed, a comprehensive care plan is developed, and services are managed and monitored by an identified care coordinator.

[8]According to the Case Management Society of America, case management is defined as a collaborative process of assessment, planning, facilitation, and advocacy for options and services to meet an individual's health needs through communication and available resources to promote quality, cost-effective outcomes.

have implemented the RCP within their existing wounded warrior programs.[9]

As a result of these multiple efforts, many recovering servicemembers and veterans are enrolled in more than one care coordination or case management program, and they may have multiple care coordinators and case managers, potentially duplicating agencies' efforts and reducing the effectiveness and efficiency of the assistance they provide. For example, recovering servicemembers and veterans who have a care coordinator also may be enrolled in one or more of the multiple DOD or VA programs that provide case management services to "seriously" and "severely" wounded, ill, and injured servicemembers, veterans, and their families. These programs include the military services' wounded warrior programs and VA's Operation Enduring Freedom/Operation Iraqi Freedom Care Management Program, among others.

We found that inadequate information exchange and poor coordination between these programs have resulted in not only duplication of effort, but confusion and frustration for enrollees, particularly when case managers and care coordinators duplicate or contradict one another's efforts. For example, an FRCP coordinator told us that in one instance there were five case managers working on the same life insurance issue for an individual. In another example, an FRCP coordinator and an RCP coordinator were not aware the other was involved in coordinating care for the same servicemember and had unknowingly established conflicting recovery goals for this individual. In this case, a servicemember with multiple amputations was advised by his FRCP coordinator to separate from the military in order to receive needed services from VA, whereas his RCP coordinator set a goal of remaining on active duty. These conflicting goals caused considerable confusion for this servicemember and his family.

DOD and VA have been unsuccessful in jointly developing options for improved collaboration and potential integration of the FRCP and RCP care coordination programs, although they have made a number of attempts to do so. Despite the identification of various options, no final decisions to revamp, merge, or eliminate programs have been agreed upon.

---

[9]The Navy, Air Force, and Marine Corps have all implemented the RCP within their existing wounded warrior programs. The Army and the U.S. Special Operations Command provide services that meet the requirements of the RCP, although they did not specifically implement this program.

The need for better collaboration and integration extends beyond the FRCP and RCP to also encompass other DOD and VA case management programs, such as DOD's wounded warrior programs that also serve seriously and severely wounded, ill, and injured servicemembers and veterans. In October 2011, we recommended that the Secretaries of Defense and Veterans Affairs direct the co-chairs of the Senior Oversight Committee to expeditiously develop and implement a plan to strengthen functional integration across all DOD and VA care coordination and case management programs that serve recovering servicemembers, veterans, and their families, including—but not limited to—the FRCP and RCP.[10] DOD and VA provided technical comments on the report, but neither specifically commented on our recommendation. We plan to track the extent to which progress has been made to address our recommendation.

- *Information technology investment management*: OMB reported that in fiscal year 2011, there were approximately 7,200 information technology (IT) investments totaling at least $79 billion. OMB provides guidance to agencies on how to report on their IT investments and requires agencies to identify each investment by a single functional category and sub-category. These categorizations are intended to enable OMB and others to analyze investments with similar functions, as well as identify and analyze potentially duplicative investments across agencies. We found that DOD and the Department of Energy (DOE) need to address potentially duplicative IT investments to avoid investing in unnecessary systems.

  In February 2012, we completed a review that examined the 3 largest categories of IT investments within DOD, DOE, and the Department of Homeland Security (DHS) and found that although the departments use various investment review processes to identify duplicative investments, 37 of our sample of 810 investments were potentially duplicative at DOD and DOE.[11] These investments account for about $1.2 billion in IT spending for fiscal years 2007 through 2012 for these two agencies. We found that DOD and DOE had recently initiated specific plans to address

---

[10]GAO, *DOD and VA Health Care: Action Needed to Strengthen Integration across Care Coordination and Case Management Programs*, GAO-12-129T (Washington, D.C.: Oct. 6, 2011).

[11]GAO, *Information Technology: Departments of Defense and Energy Need to Address Potentially Duplicative Investments*, GAO-12-241 (Washington, D.C.: Feb. 17, 2012).

potential duplication in many of the investments we identified—such as plans to consolidate or eliminate systems—but these initiatives had not yet led to the consolidation or elimination of duplicative investments or functionality.

In addition, while we did not identify any potentially duplicative investments at DHS within our sample, DHS officials have independently identified several duplicative investments and systems. DHS has plans to further consolidate systems within these investments by 2014, which it expects to produce approximately $41 million in cost savings. DHS officials have also identified 38 additional systems that they have determined to be duplicative.

Further complicating agencies' ability to identify and eliminate duplicative investments is that investments are, in certain cases, misclassified by function. For example, one of DHS's Federal Emergency Management Agency (FEMA) investments was initially categorized within the Employee Performance Management sub-function, but DHS agreed that this investment should be assigned to the Human Resources Development sub-function. Proper categorization is necessary in order to analyze and identify duplicative IT investments, both within and across agencies.

In February 2012, we recommended that the Secretaries of DOD and DOE direct their Chief Information Officers to utilize existing transparency mechanisms to report on the results of their efforts to identify and eliminate, where appropriate, each potentially duplicative investment that we identified, as well as any other duplicative investments. The agencies agreed with our recommendation. We also recommended that DOD, DOE, and DHS correct the miscategorizations of the investments we identified and ensure that investments are correctly categorized in agency submissions, which would enhance the agencies' ability to identify opportunities to consolidate or eliminate duplicative investments. DOD and DHS agreed with our recommendation, but DOE disagreed that two of the four investments we identified were miscategorized, explaining that its categorizations reflect funding considerations. However, OMB guidance indicates that investments should be classified according to their intended purpose. Consequently, we believe the recommendation is warranted.

- *Department of Homeland Security grants*: From fiscal years 2002 through 2011, FEMA, under DHS, allocated about $20.3 billion to grant recipients through four specific programs (the State Homeland Security Program, Urban Areas Security Initiative, Port Security Grant Program, and Transit

Security Grant Program) to enhance the capacity of states, localities, and other entities, such as ports or transit agencies, to prevent, respond to, and recover from a terrorism incident. We found that DHS needs better project information and coordination to identify and mitigate potential unnecessary duplication among four overlapping grant programs.

In February 2012, we identified multiple factors that contributed to the risk of FEMA potentially funding unnecessarily duplicative projects across these four grant programs. These factors include overlap among grant recipients, goals, and geographic locations, combined with differing levels of information that FEMA had available regarding grant projects and recipients.[12] We also reported that FEMA lacked a process to coordinate application reviews across the four grant programs and grant applications were reviewed separately by program and were not compared across each other to determine where possible unnecessary duplication may occur. Specifically, FEMA's Homeland Security Grant Program branch administered the Urban Areas Security Initiative and State Homeland Security Program while the Transportation Infrastructure Security branch administered the Port Security Grant Program and Transit Security Grant Program. We and the DHS Inspector General have concluded that coordinating the review of grant projects internally would give FEMA more complete information about applications across the four grant programs, which could help FEMA identify and mitigate the risk of unnecessary duplication across grant applications.[13]

We also identified actions FEMA could take to identify and mitigate any unnecessary duplication in these programs, such as collecting more complete project information as well as exploring opportunities to enhance FEMA's internal coordination and administration of the programs. We suggested that Congress may wish to consider requiring DHS to report on the results of its efforts to identify and prevent duplication within and across the four grant programs, and consider these results when making future funding decisions for these programs.

---

[12]GAO, *Homeland Security: DHS Needs Better Project Information and Coordination among Four Overlapping Grant Programs,* GAO-12-303 (Washington, D.C.: Feb. 28, 2012).

[13]Department of Homeland Security Office of Inspector General, *Efficacy of DHS Grant Programs,* OIG-1069 (Washington, D.C.: Mar. 22, 2010).

GAO-12-449T

- *Science, Technology, Engineering, and Math education programs*:
  Federal agencies obligated $3.1 billion in fiscal year 2010 on Science,
  Technology, Engineering, and Mathematics (STEM) education programs.
  These programs can serve an important role both by helping to prepare
  students and teachers for careers in STEM fields and by enhancing the
  nation's global competitiveness. In addition to the federal effort, state and
  local governments, universities and colleges, and the private sector have
  also developed programs that provide opportunities for students to pursue
  STEM education and occupations. Recently, both Congress and the
  administration have called for a more strategic and effective approach to
  the federal government's investment in STEM education. For example,
  Congress directed the Office of Science and Technology Policy, within
  the Executive Office of the President, to establish a committee under its
  component National Science and Technology Council to, among other
  things, develop a 5-year governmentwide STEM education strategic plan
  and identify areas of duplication among federal programs.[14] We found
  that strategic planning is needed to better manage overlapping programs
  across multiple agencies.

  In January 2012, we reported that 173 of the 209 (83 percent) STEM
  education programs administered by 13 federal agencies overlapped to
  some degree with at least 1 other program in that they offered similar
  services to target groups—such as K-12 students, postsecondary
  students, K-12 teachers, and college faculty and staff—to achieve similar
  objectives.[15] These overlapping programs largely resulted from federal
  efforts to both create and expand programs across many agencies in an
  effort to improve STEM education and increase the number of students
  going into related fields. Overlapping programs can lead to individuals
  and institutions being eligible for similar services in similar STEM fields
  offered through multiple programs. For example, 177 of the 209 programs
  (85 percent) were primarily intended to serve two or more target groups.
  Overlap can frustrate federal officials' efforts to administer programs in a
  comprehensive manner, limit the ability of decision makers to determine
  which programs are most cost-effective, and ultimately increase program
  administrative costs.

---

[14]Pub. L. No. 111-358, § 101, 124 Stat. 3982, 3984 (2011).

[15]GAO, *Science, Technology, Engineering, and Mathematics Education: Strategic
Planning Needed to Better Manage Overlapping Programs across Multiple Agencies*,
GAO-12-108 (Washington, D.C.: Jan. 20, 2012).

Even when programs overlap, the services they provide and the populations they serve may differ in meaningful ways and would therefore not necessarily be duplicative. There may be important differences between the specific STEM field of focus and the program's stated goals. For example, we identified 31 programs that provided scholarships or fellowships to doctoral students in the field of physics. However, one program's goal was to increase environmental literacy related to estuaries and coastal watersheds while another program focused on supporting education in nuclear science, engineering, and related trades. In addition, programs may be primarily intended to serve different specific populations within a given target group. Of the 34 programs providing services to K-12 students in the field of technology, 10 are primarily intended to serve specific underrepresented, minority, or disadvantaged groups and 2 are limited geographically to individual cities or universities.

However, little is known about the effectiveness of federal STEM education programs. Since 2005, when we first reported on this issue, we have found that the majority of programs have not conducted comprehensive evaluations of how well their programs are working. Agency and program officials would benefit from guidance and information sharing within and across agencies about what is working and how to best evaluate programs. This would not only help to improve individual program performance, but could also inform agency- and governmentwide decisions about which programs should continue to be funded. Furthermore, although the National Science and Technology Council is in the process of developing a governmentwide strategic plan for STEM education, we found that agencies have not used outcome measures for STEM programs in a way that is clearly reflected in their own performance plans and performance reports—key strategic planning documents. The absence of clear links between the programs and agencies' planning documents may hinder decision makers' ability to assess how agencies' STEM efforts contribute to agencywide performance goals and the overall federal STEM effort.

We reported in January 2012 that numerous opportunities exist to improve the planning for STEM programs. For example, we recommended that the National Science and Technology Council develop guidance for how agencies can better incorporate governmentwide STEM education strategic plan goals and their STEM education efforts into their respective performance plans and reports, as well as determining the types of evaluations that may be feasible and appropriate for different types of STEM education programs. We also recommended that the National Science and Technology Council work with agencies, through the strategic planning process, to identify STEM education programs that might be candidates for consolidation or elimination. OMB stated that our recommendations are critical to improving the provision of STEM education across the federal government. In separate comments, the Office of Science and Technology Policy said its own analysis of STEM education programs identified no duplicative programs and where it identified overlapping programs it found that some program characteristics differed. As an illustration, the Office of Science and Technology Policy explained that there could be two STEM education programs, one that worked with inner city children in New York City and another with rural children in North Dakota. We agree that it may be important to serve both of these populations, but it is not clear that two separate administrative structures are necessary to ensure both populations are served. The Office of Science and Technology Policy said it would address our recommendations in the 5-year Federal STEM Education Strategic Plan, which will be released in spring 2012. Furthermore, the President's Fiscal Year 2013 budget established STEM education programs as one of fourteen cross-agency priority goals. These goals are intended to enhance progress in areas needing more cross-government collaboration.

- *Coordination of space system organizations*: U.S. government space systems—such as the Global Positioning System (GPS) and space-based weather systems—provide a wide range of capabilities to a large number of users, including the federal government, U.S. businesses and citizens, and other countries. Space systems are usually very expensive, often costing billions of dollars to acquire. More than $25 billion a year is appropriated to agencies for developing space systems. These systems typically take a long time to develop, and often consist of multiple components, including satellites, ground control stations, terminals, and user equipment. Moreover, the nation's satellites are put into orbit by rockets that can cost more than $100 million per launch. We have found that costs of space programs tend to increase significantly from initial cost estimates. A variety of agencies, such as the Federal Aviation Administration, the National Oceanic and Atmospheric Administration, and DHS rely on government space systems to execute their missions, but responsibilities for acquiring space systems are diffused across various DOD organizations as well as the intelligence community and the National Aeronautics and Space Administration. Fragmented leadership has led to program challenges and potential duplication in developing multi-billion dollar space systems. In some cases, problems with these systems have been so severe that acquisitions were either canceled or the needed capabilities were severely delayed.

Fragmented leadership and lack of a single authority in overseeing the acquisition of space programs have created challenges for optimally acquiring, developing, and deploying new space systems. This fragmentation is problematic not only because of a lack of coordination that has led to delays in fielding systems, but also because no one person or organization is held accountable for balancing governmentwide needs against wants, resolving conflicts and ensuring coordination among the many organizations involved with space acquisitions, and ensuring that resources are directed where they are most needed. For example, we reported in April 2009 that the coordination of GPS satellites and user equipment segments is not adequately synchronized due to funding shifts and diffuse leadership in the program, likely leading to numerous years of missed opportunities to utilize new capabilities.[16] DOD has taken some steps to better coordinate the GPS segments by creating the Space and Intelligence Office within the Office of the Under Secretary of Defense for Acquisition, Technology, and Logistics and conducting enterprise level reviews of the GPS program. However, DOD has not yet established a single authority responsible for ensuring that all GPS segments, including user equipment, are synchronized to the maximum extent practicable.

DOD has also undertaken a number of initiatives to improve leadership over defense space acquisitions, but these actions have not been in place long enough to determine whether acquisition outcomes will improve. Moreover, the initiatives do not extend to the space activities across the government. We and others, including the Commission to Assess United States National Security Space Management and Organization, have previously recommended a number of changes to the leadership of the space community and have consistently reported that a lack of strong, centralized leadership has led to inefficiencies and other problems. But the question as to what office or leadership structure above the department level would be effective and appropriate for coordinating all U.S. government space programs and setting priorities has not been addressed.

We have suggested that OMB work with the National Security Council to assess whether a governmentwide oversight body for space acquisitions is needed. OMB agreed that coordinating space activities across the U.S.

---

[16]GAO, *Global Positioning System: Significant Challenges in Sustaining and Upgrading Widely Used Capabilities*, GAO-09-325 (Washington, D.C.: Apr. 30, 2009).

government has been and continues to be a major challenge, but is concerned that our recommendation would add an extra layer of space bureaucracy on top of ongoing coordination efforts as well as additional costs and possible confusion regarding roles and authorities among the existing mechanisms. We believe that the recommendation is sufficiently flexible to allow for an implementation approach that would address these concerns.

- *Defense Language and Culture Training*: DOD has emphasized the importance of developing language skills and knowledge of foreign cultures within its forces to meet the needs of current and future military operations and it has invested millions of dollars to provide language and culture training to thousands of servicemembers, including those deploying to ongoing operations. For example, we estimated that DOD invested about $266 million for fiscal years 2005 through 2011 to provide general purpose forces with training support, such as classroom instruction, computer-based training, and training aids. We found that DOD has not developed an integrated approach to reduce fragmentation in the military services' language and culture training approaches and overlap in the content of training products acquired by the military services and other organizations.

  In May 2011, we reported that language and culture training within DOD is not provided through a single department- or servicewide program, but rather multiple DOD organizations oversee the development and acquisition of language and culture training and related products and deliver training.[17] We recommended that the Office of the Under Secretary of Defense for Personnel and Readiness establish internal mechanisms to assist the department in reaching consensus with the military services and other DOD entities on training priorities, synchronize the development of service- and departmentwide plans with the budget process, and guide efforts to monitor progress. DOD agreed with our recommendation.

  We also found that the military services have not fully coordinated efforts to develop and acquire language and culture training products. As a result, the services have acquired overlapping and potentially duplicative

---

[17]GAO, *Military Training: Additional Actions Needed to Improve Planning and Coordination of Army and Marine Corps Language and Culture Training*, GAO-11-456 (Washington, D.C.: May 26, 2011).

products, such as reference materials containing country- or region-specific cultural information and computer software or web-based training programs that can be used within a distributed learning training environment. To illustrate, we analyzed 18 DOD language and culture training products and found that the content overlapped to some extent with at least one other training product. For Afghan languages, DOD invested in at least five products that were intended to build basic foreign language skills or specific language skills needed to perform military tasks.

We suggested that the Office of the Under Secretary of Defense for Personnel and Readiness and the military services designate organizational responsibility and a supporting process to inventory and evaluate existing language and culture products and plans for additional investments, eliminate any unnecessary overlap and duplication, and adjust resources accordingly, as well as take steps to develop and contract for new products that can be used by more than one military service. DOD agreed that departmentwide coordination efforts could be improved and noted that our analysis would be useful in targeting specific areas for improvement.

- *Federal facility risk assessments*: Federal facilities continue to be vulnerable to terrorist attacks and other acts of violence, as evidenced by the 2010 attacks on the IRS building in Austin, Texas, and the federal courthouse in Las Vegas, Nevada, which resulted in loss of life. DHS's Federal Protective Service (FPS) is the primary federal agency responsible for providing physical security and law enforcement services—including conducting risk assessments—for the approximately 9,000 federal facilities under the control and custody of the General Services Administration. We found that agencies are making duplicate payments for facility risk assessments by completing their own assessments, while also paying DHS for assessments that the department is not performing.

  We reported in June 2008 and also have recently found that multiple federal agencies are expending additional resources to assess their own facilities; although, according to an FPS official, the agency received $236 million from federal agencies for risk assessments and other security services in fiscal year 2011.[18] For example, an IRS official stated that IRS completed risk assessments based on concerns about risks unique to its mission for approximately 65 facilities that it also paid FPS to assess. Additionally, Environmental Protection Agency officials said that the agency has conducted its own assessments based on concerns with the quality and thoroughness of FPS's assessments. These assessments are conducted by teams of contractors and agency employees, cost an estimated $6,000, and can take a few days to a week to complete.

FPS's planned risk assessment tool is intended to provide FPS with the capability to assess risks at federal facilities based on threat, vulnerability, and consequence; and track countermeasures to mitigate those risks, but it is unclear if the tool will help minimize duplication. According to an official, FPS planned to use its Risk Assessment and Management Program to complete assessments of about 700 federal facilities in fiscal year 2010 and 2,500 facilities in fiscal year 2011. However, as we reported in July 2011, FPS experienced cost overruns, schedule delays, and operational issues with developing this program and as a result the agency could not use it to complete risk assessments.[19] We found that since November 2009, the agency has only completed four risk assessments using its Risk Assessment and Management Program.

We identified several steps that DHS could take to address duplication in FPS's risk assessments. For example, in July 2011 we recommended that DHS develop interim solutions for completing risk assessments while addressing challenges with the Risk Assessment and Management Program. In addition, in February 2012, we suggested DHS work with federal agencies to determine their reasons for duplicating the activities included in FPS's risk assessments and identify measures to reduce this duplication. DHS agreed with our July 2011 recommendation and has begun taking action to address it, but did not comment on the action we identified in February 2012.

---

[18]GAO, *Homeland Security: The Federal Protective Service Faces Several Challenges That Hamper Its Ability to Protect Federal Facilities*, GAO-08-683 (Washington, D.C.: June 11, 2008).

[19]GAO, *Federal Protective Service: Actions Needed to Resolve Delays and Inadequate Oversight Issues with FPS's Risk Assessment and Management Program*, GAO-11-705R (Washington, D.C.: July 15, 2011).

Our 2012 annual report also summarized 19 areas—beyond those directly related to duplication, overlap, or fragmentation—describing other opportunities for agencies or Congress to consider taking action that could either reduce the cost of government operations or enhance revenue collection for the Treasury. These cost saving and revenue-enhancing opportunities also span a wide range of federal government agencies and mission areas (see table 2).

Table 2: Cost-Saving or Revenue-Enhancing Opportunities Identified

Mission	Areas identified
Defense	33. **Air Force Food Service:** The Air Force has opportunities to achieve millions of dollars in cost savings annually by reviewing and renegotiating food service contracts, where appropriate, to better align with the needs of installations.
	34. **Defense Headquarters:** The Department of Defense should review and identify further opportunities for consolidating or reducing the size of headquarters organizations.
	35. **Defense Real Property:** Ensuring the receipt of fair market value for leasing underused real property and monitoring administrative costs could help the military services' enhanced use lease programs realize intended financial benefits.
	36. **Military Health Care Costs:** To help achieve significant projected cost savings and other performance goals, DOD needs to complete, implement, and monitor detailed plans for each of its approved health care initiatives.
	37. **Overseas Defense Posture:** The Department of Defense could reduce costs of its Pacific region presence by developing comprehensive cost information and re-examining alternatives to planned initiatives.
	38. **Navy's Information Technology Enterprise Network:** Better informed decisions are needed to ensure a more cost-effective acquisition approach for the Navy's Next Generation Enterprise Network.
Economic development	39. **Auto Recovery Office:** Unless the Secretary of Labor can demonstrate how the Auto Recovery Office has uniquely assisted auto communities, Congress may wish to consider prohibiting the Department of Labor from spending any of its appropriations on the Auto Recovery Office and instead require that the department direct the funds to other federal programs that provide funding directly to affected communities.
Energy	40. **Excess Uranium Inventories:** Marketing the Department of Energy's excess uranium could provide billions in revenue for the government.
General government	41. **General Services Administration Schedules Contracts Fee Rates:** Re-evaluating fee rates on the General Services Administration's Multiple Award Schedules contracts could result in significant cost savings governmentwide.
	42. **U.S. Currency:** Legislation replacing the $1 note with a $1 coin would provide a significant financial benefit to the government over time.
	43. **Federal User Fees:** Regularly reviewing federal user fees and charges can help the Congress and federal agencies identify opportunities to address inconsistent federal funding approaches and enhance user financing, thereby reducing reliance on general fund appropriations.
	44. **Internal Revenue Service Enforcement Efforts:** Enhancing the Internal Revenue Service's enforcement and service capabilities can help reduce the gap between taxes owed and paid by collecting billions in tax revenue and facilitating voluntary compliance.
Health	45. **Medicare Advantage Payment:** The Centers for Medicare and Medicaid Services could achieve billions of dollars in additional savings by better adjusting for differences between Medicare Advantage plans and traditional Medicare providers in the reporting of beneficiary diagnoses.

Mission	Areas identified
	46. **Medicare and Medicaid Fraud Detection Systems:** The Centers for Medicare and Medicaid Services needs to ensure widespread use of technology to help detect and recover billions of dollars of improper payments of claims and better position itself to determine and measure financial and other benefits of its systems.
Homeland security/Law enforcement	47. **Border Security:** Delaying proposed investments for future acquisitions of border surveillance technology until the Department of Homeland Security better defines and measures benefits and estimates life-cycle costs could help ensure the most effective use of future program funding.
	48. **Passenger Aviation Security Fees:** Options for adjusting the passenger aviation security fee could further offset billions of dollars in civil aviation security costs.
	49. **Immigration Inspection Fee:** The air passenger immigration inspection user fee should be reviewed and adjusted to fully recover the cost of the air passenger immigration inspection activities conducted by Department of Homeland Security's U.S. Immigration and Customs Enforcement and U.S. Customs and Border Protection rather than using general fund appropriations.
International affairs	50. **Iraq Security Funding:** When considering new funding requests to train and equip Iraqi security forces, Congress should consider the government of Iraq's financial resources, which afford it the ability to contribute more toward the cost of Iraq's security.
Social services	51. **Domestic Disaster Assistance:** The Federal Emergency Management Agency could reduce the costs to the federal government related to major disasters declared by the President by updating the principal indicator on which disaster funding decisions are based and better measuring a state's capacity to respond without federal assistance.

Source: GAO-12-342SP.

Examples of opportunities for agencies or Congress to consider taking action that could either reduce the cost of government operations or enhance revenue collections include:

- *Air Force food service*: According to Air Force officials, most Air Force installations have their own individual contracts for food service, with a total cost of approximately $150 million per year for all Air Force installations. We found that the Air Force has opportunities to reduce its overall food service costs by millions of dollars annually by reviewing food service contracts and adjusting them, when appropriate, to better meet the needs of its installations, including aligning labor needs with the actual number of meals served by the dining facilities.

The Air Force recently undertook an initiative to improve food service at six pilot installations, with intentions to eventually expand this initiative to more Air Force installations. Among other intended outcomes, Air Force officials stated that the first group of pilot installations achieved cost savings when compared to their previous contracts while also increasing hours of operation in the dining facilities and serving an additional 500,000 meals per year. We compared the estimated amount of food service labor at the six pilot installations under prior contracts to the projected work schedules under the initiative and found that by adjusting staffing levels for contractor staff at dining facilities, the contractor reduced the total number of labor hours at five of the six pilot installations by 53 percent. For example, at one installation, the number of estimated labor hours decreased from approximately 2,042 hours per week to 920. For the sixth installation where the labor hours did not decrease, the Air Force Audit Agency had recently conducted a review that found that the number of food service personnel did not align with workload estimates. As a result, the Air Force renegotiated its workload estimates and pay rates, resulting in savings of approximately $77,000 annually.

During our review, we discussed the potential opportunity for achieving additional savings by reviewing staffing levels at other installations outside of the initiative with Air Force officials. As a result, the Air Force issued a memorandum directing a review of existing food service contracts to determine if the contracts meet current mission needs. The memorandum indicated that special attention must be given to whether the food service contract workload estimates were properly aligned with the actual number of meals served. In July 2011, we recommended that the Secretary of the Air Force monitor the actions taken in response to the direction to review food service contracts, and take actions, as appropriate, to ensure that cost-savings measures are implemented.[20] According to Air Force officials, eight installations have recently reviewed and renegotiated their food service contracts for a total savings of over $2.5 million per year. The potential exists for other installations that rely on contracts to meet their food service needs to achieve similar financial benefits. For example, the Air Force has requested that each of its installations conduct a 100 percent review of existing food service contracts to determine if their current contract workload estimates meet current mission needs or if the contracts require modification. In addition, the Office of the Secretary of Defense planned to share the results of the Air Force's review of its food service labor costs to achieve cost savings with the other military services.

- *Navy information technology network*: In 2007, the Navy established the Next Generation Enterprise Network program (NGEN) to replace and improve the Navy Marine Corps Intranet. According to the President's fiscal year 2012 budget request, the NGEN program has spent about $434 million on work associated with the transition from the Navy Marine

---

[20]GAO, *Defense Management: Actions Needed to Improve Management of Air Force's Food Transformation Initiative*, GAO-11-676 (Washington, D.C.: July 26, 2011).

Corps Intranet. The Navy estimated that NGEN would cost approximately $50 billion to develop, operate, and maintain through fiscal year 2025. We found that better informed decisions were needed to ensure a more cost-effective acquisition approach for the Navy's NGEN program.

We reported in March 2011 that the Navy selected an approach that was not considered as part of its analysis of alternatives and that it estimated would cost at least $4.7 billion more than any of the four assessed alternatives.[21] In addition, we reported that the Navy's schedule for NGEN also did not provide a reliable basis for program execution because it did not adequately satisfy key schedule estimating best practices, such as establishing the critical path (the sequence of activities that, if delayed, impacts the planned completion date of the project) and assigning resources to all work activities. We also found that the Navy's acquisition decisions were not always performance- or risk-based. In particular, senior executives approved the NGEN program's continuing progress in the face of known performance shortfalls and risks.

To address these weaknesses, we recommended in March 2011 that the Navy limit further investment in NGEN until it conducts an immediate interim review to reconsider the selected acquisition approach. We also identified an additional action that the Navy could take to facilitate implementation of the approach resulting from this review by ensuring that the NGEN schedule reflects key schedule estimating practices and future program reviews and decisions fully reflect the program's performance and exposure to risk. DOD agreed with our recommendation to ensure that future NGEN acquisition reviews and decisions fully reflect the state of the program's performance and its exposure to risks. The department did not agree with our recommendation to reconsider its acquisition approach; however, the Navy is currently in the process of reviewing and making changes to the NGEN acquisition strategy. We are undertaking work that will assess the extent to which the Navy has conducted its interim review to reconsider its acquisition approach and evaluate the revised strategy.

- *DOD health care costs*: DOD spends billions of dollars annually on its worldwide healthcare system. Currently, health care costs constitute nearly

---

[21]GAO, *Information Technology: Better Informed Decision Making Needed on Navy's Next Generation Enterprise Network Acquisition*, GAO-11-150 (Washington, D.C.: Mar. 11, 2011).

10 percent of DOD's baseline budget request. For its fiscal year 2012 budget, according to DOD documentation, DOD received $52.7 billion[22] to provide health care to approximately 9.6 million active duty servicemembers, reservists, retirees, and their dependents. DOD recognizes that it must address the rate at which health care costs are rising and has stated that it intends to continue to develop health care initiatives that will improve the quality and standard of care, while reducing growth in overall costs.[23] Our ongoing work has found that DOD has identified 11 initiatives intended to slow the rise in its health care costs, but it has not fully applied results-oriented management practices to its efforts or an overall monitoring process, which limits its effectiveness in implementing these initiatives and achieving related cost savings goals.

DOD's initiatives consist primarily of changes to clinical and business practices in areas ranging from primary care to psychological health to purchased care reimbursement practices. Partly in response to our ongoing work assessing DOD's management of its initiatives, the department has taken some initial steps toward managing their implementation by developing a number of high-level, non-monetary metrics and corresponding goals for each strategic initiative, and other management tools, such as implementation plans that will include key elements such as investment costs and savings estimates. However, DOD currently has completed only one implementation plan, which contains the one available cost savings estimate among all the initiatives. Without completing its plans and incorporating elements such as problem definitions, resources needed, goals, performance measures, and cost estimates into them, DOD will not be fully aware if these initiatives are achieving projected cost savings and other performance goals.

In addition, DOD has not completed the implementation of an overall monitoring process across its portfolio of initiatives for overseeing the initiatives' progress or identified accountable officials and their roles and responsibilities for all of its initiatives. DOD's 2007 *Task Force on the Future of Military Health Care* noted that the current Military Health

---

[22]DOD's fiscal year 2012 budget of $52.7 billion for its Unified Medical Budget includes $32.5 billion for the Defense Health Program, $8.3 billion for military personnel, $1.1 billion for military construction, and $10.8 billion for the Medicare Eligible Retiree Health Care Fund. The total excludes overseas contingency operations funds and other transfers.

[23]DOD, *Quadrennial Defense Review Report*, February 2010.

System does not function as a fully integrated health care system.[24] For example, while the Assistant Secretary of Defense for Health Affairs controls the Defense Health Program budget, the services directly supervise their medical personnel and manage their military treatment facilities. Therefore, as Military Health System leaders develop and implement their plans to control rising health care costs, they will need to work across multiple authorities and areas of responsibility. Until DOD fully implements a military-wide mechanism to monitor progress and identify accountable officials, including their roles and responsibilities across its portfolio of initiatives, DOD may be hindered in its ability to achieve a more cost-efficient military health system.

In order to enhance its efforts to manage rising health care costs and demonstrate sustained leadership commitment for achieving the performance goals of the Military Health System's strategic initiatives, we plan to recommend as part of our ongoing work that DOD complete and fully implement detailed implementation plans for each of the approved health care initiatives in a manner consistent with results-oriented management practices, such as the inclusion of upfront investment costs and cost savings estimates; and complete the implementation of an overall monitoring process across its portfolio of initiatives for overseeing the initiatives' progress and identifying accountable officials and their roles and responsibilities for all of its initiatives. We believe that DOD may realize projected cost savings and other performance goals by taking these actions to help ensure the successful implementation of its cost savings initiatives. Given that DOD identified these initiatives as steps to slow the rapidly growing costs of its medical program, if implemented these initiatives could potentially save DOD millions of dollars. DOD generally agreed with our planned recommendations.

- *Excess uranium inventories*: DOE maintains large inventories of depleted and natural uranium that it no longer requires for nuclear weapons or fuel for naval nuclear propulsion reactors. We reported in March and April 2008 and again in June 2011 that under certain conditions, the federal

---

[24]Defense Health Board, *Task Force on the Future of Military Health Care*, December 2007.

government could generate billions of dollars by marketing inventories of excess uranium to commercial power plants to use in their reactors.[25]

Specifically, we identified options that DOE could take to market the excess uranium inventories for commercial use. For example, DOE could contract to re-enrich inventories of depleted uranium hexafluoride (a by-product of the uranium enrichment process), consisting of hundreds of thousands of metric tons of material that are stored at DOE's uranium enrichment plants. Although DOE would have to pay for processing, the resulting re-enriched uranium could be potentially sold if the sales price of the uranium exceeded processing costs. DOE could also pursue an option of selling the depleted uranium inventory "as-is". This approach would require DOE to obtain the appropriate statutory authority to sell depleted uranium in its current unprocessed form. Firms such as nuclear power utilities and enrichment companies might find it cost effective to purchase the uranium and re-enrich it as a source of nuclear fuel.

If executed in accordance with federal law, DOE sales of natural uranium could generate additional revenue for the government. Natural uranium on its own cannot fuel nuclear reactors and weapons. Rather, it is shipped to a conversion facility, where it is converted for the enrichment process. We reported in September 2011 that in 7 transactions executed since 2009 DOE has, in effect, sold nearly 1,900 metric tons of natural uranium into the market, using a contractor as a sales agent, to fund environmental cleanup services.[26] DOE characterized these sales as barter transactions—exchanges of services (environmental cleanup work) for materials (uranium). While DOE received no cash directly from the transactions, it allowed its contractor to keep cash from the sales, which DOE would otherwise have owed to the United States Treasury. Because federal law requires an official or agent of the government receiving money for the government from any source to deposit the money in the

---

[25]See GAO, *Nuclear Material: DOE Has Several Potential Options for Dealing with Depleted Uranium Tails, Each of Which Could Benefit the Government*, GAO-08-606R (Washington, D.C.: Mar. 31, 2008); *Nuclear Material: Several Potential Options for Dealing with DOE's Depleted Uranium Tails Could Benefit the Government*, GAO-08-613T (Washington, D.C.: Apr. 3, 2008); and *Nuclear Material: DOE's Depleted Uranium Tails Could Be a Source of Revenue for the Government*, GAO-11-752T (Washington, D.C.: June 13, 2011).

[26]GAO, *Excess Uranium Inventories: Clarifying DOE's Disposition Options Could Help Avoid Further Legal Violations*, GAO-11-846 (Washington, D.C.: Sept. 26, 2011).

Treasury, we found that these transactions violated the miscellaneous receipts statute.

We have reported that congressional action may be needed to overcome legal obstacles to the pursuit of certain options for the sale of depleted and natural uranium. Specifically, our March 2008 report suggested that Congress may wish to explicitly provide direction about whether and how DOE may sell or transfer depleted uranium in its current form. Our September 2011 report suggested that if Congress sees merit in using the proceeds from the barter, transfer, or sale of federal uranium assets to pay for environmental cleanup work, it could consider providing DOE with explicit authority to barter excess uranium and to retain the proceeds from these transactions. We also suggested that Congress could direct DOE to sell uranium for cash and make those proceeds available by appropriation for environmental cleanup work.

Congress has taken some actions in response to our work. For example, the Consolidated Appropriations Act, 2012, among other things, requires the Secretary of Energy to provide congressional appropriations committees with information on the transfer, sale, barter, distribution, or other provision of uranium in any form and an estimate of the uranium value along with the expected recipient of the material. The Consolidated Appropriations Act, 2012 also requires the Secretary to submit a report evaluating the economic feasibility of re-enriching depleted uranium.

- *Medicare and Medicaid fraud detection systems*: We have designated Medicare and Medicaid as high-risk programs, in part due to their susceptibility to improper payments—estimated to be about $65 billion in fiscal year 2011. To integrate data about all types of Medicare and Medicaid claims and improve its ability to detect fraud, waste, and abuse in these programs, the Centers for Medicare and Medicaid Services (CMS) initiated two information technology programs—the Integrated Data Repository, which is intended to provide a centralized repository of claims data for all Medicare and Medicaid programs, and One Program Integrity, a set of tools that enables CMS contractors and staff to access and analyze data retrieved from the repository. According to CMS officials, the systems are expected to provide financial benefits of more than $21 billion by the end of fiscal year 2015. We found that CMS needs to ensure widespread use of technology to help detect and recover billions of dollars of improper payments of claims and better position itself to determine and measure financial and other benefits of its systems.

We reported in June 2011 that CMS had developed and begun using both systems, but was not yet positioned to identify, measure, or track benefits realized from these programs.[27] For example, although in use since 2006, the Integrated Data Repository did not have Medicaid claims data or information from other CMS systems that store and process data related to the entry, correction, and adjustment of claims due to funding and other technical issues. These data are needed to help analysts prevent improper payments. Program officials told us that they had begun incorporating these data in September 2011 and planned to make them available to program integrity analysts in spring 2012. Regarding Medicaid data, agency officials stated that they did not account for difficulties associated with integrating data from the various types and formats of data stored in disparate state systems or develop reliable schedules for its efforts to incorporate these data. In particular, program officials did not consider certain risks and obstacles, such as technical challenges, as they developed schedules for implementing the Integrated Data Repository. Lacking reliable schedules, CMS may face additional delays in making available all the data that are needed to support enhanced program integrity efforts.

In addition, CMS had not trained its broad community of analysts to use the One Program Integrity system because of delays introduced by a redesign of initial training plans that were found to be insufficient. Specifically, program officials planned for 639 analysts to be using the system by the end of fiscal year 2010; however only 41—less than 7 percent—were actively using it as of October 2010. Because of these delays, the initial use of the system was limited to a small number of CMS staff and contractors. In updating the status of the training efforts in November 2011, although we did not validate these data, CMS officials reported that a total of 215 program integrity analysts had been trained and were using the system. However, program officials had not finalized plans and schedules for training all intended users.

In June 2011, we recommended that CMS take a number of actions to help ensure the program's success toward achieving the billions of dollars in financial benefits that program integrity officials projected, such as

---

[27]GAO, *Fraud Detection Systems: Centers for Medicare and Medicaid Services Needs to Ensure More Widespread Use*, GAO-11-475 (Washington, D.C.: June 30, 2011).

finalizing plans and reliable schedules for incorporating additional data into the Integrated Data Repository and conducting training for all analysts who are intended to use the One Program Integrity system. CMS agreed with our recommendations and identified steps the agency is taking to implement them. We plan to conduct additional work to determine whether CMS has addressed our recommendations and identified financial benefits and progress toward meeting agency goals resulting from the implementation of its fraud detection systems.

- *Medicare Advantage*: In fiscal year 2010, the federal government spent about $113 billion on the Medicare Advantage program, a private plan alternative to the original Medicare program that covers about a quarter of Medicare beneficiaries. CMS, the agency that administers Medicare, adjusts payments to Medicare Advantage plans based on the health status of each plan's enrollees. The agency could achieve billions of dollars in additional savings by better adjusting for differences between Medicare Advantage plans and traditional Medicare providers in the reporting of beneficiary diagnoses.

  CMS calculates a risk score for every beneficiary—a relative measure of health status—which is based on a beneficiary's demographic characteristics, such as age and gender, and major medical conditions. To obtain information on the medical conditions of beneficiaries in traditional Medicare, CMS generally analyzes diagnoses—numerically coded by providers into Medicare defined categories—on the claims that providers submit for payment. For beneficiaries enrolled in Medicare Advantage plans, which do not submit claims, CMS requires plans to submit diagnostic codes for each beneficiary. Analysis has shown that risk scores are higher for Medicare Advantage beneficiaries than for beneficiaries in traditional Medicare with the same characteristics.

  Medicare Advantage plans have a financial incentive to ensure that all relevant diagnoses are coded, as this can increase beneficiaries' risk scores and, ultimately, payments to the plans. Many traditional Medicare providers are paid for services rendered, and providers have less incentive to code all relevant diagnoses. Policymakers have expressed concern that risk scores for Medicare Advantage beneficiaries have grown at a faster rate than those for traditional Medicare, in part because of differences in coding diagnoses. In 2005, Congress directed CMS to analyze and adjust risk scores for differences in coding practices, and in 2010, CMS estimated that 3.41 percent of Medicare Advantage risk scores were due to differences in diagnostic coding practices. It reduced the scores by an equal percentage, thereby saving $2.7 billion.

We identified shortcomings in CMS's method for adjusting Medicare Advantage payments to reflect differences in diagnostic coding practices between Medicare Advantage and traditional Medicare. CMS did not use the most recent risk score data for its estimates; account for the increasing annual impact of coding differences over time; or account for beneficiary characteristics beyond differences in age and mortality between the Medicare Advantage and traditional Medicare populations, such as sex, Medicaid enrollment status, and beneficiary residential location. We estimated that a revised methodology that addressed these shortcomings could have saved Medicare between $1.2 billion and $3.1 billion in 2010 in addition to the $2.7 billion in savings that CMS's 3.41 percent adjustment produced. We expect that savings in future years will be greater. In January 2012, we recommended that CMS take action to help ensure appropriate payments to Medicare Advantage plans and improve the accuracy of the adjustment made for differences in coding practices over time.[28] The Department of Health and Human Services characterized our results as similar to those obtained by CMS.

- *User fees*: User fees assign part or all of the costs of federal programs and activities—the cost of providing a benefit that is above and beyond what is normally available to the general public—to readily identifiable users of those programs and activities. Regularly reviewing federal user fees and charges can help the Congress and federal agencies identify opportunities to address inconsistent federal funding approaches and enhance user financing, thereby reducing reliance on general fund appropriations.

  The Chief Financial Officers Act of 1990 (CFO Act) requires agencies to biennially review their fees and to recommend fee adjustments, as appropriate; additionally, OMB Circulars No. A-11 and No. A-25 direct agencies to discuss the results of these reviews and any resulting proposals, such as adjustments to fee rates, in the CFO annual report required by the CFO Act.[29] In 2011, we surveyed the 24 agencies covered by the CFO Act on their review of user fees. 21 of the 23 agencies that responded reported charging more than 3,600 fees and

---

[28]GAO, *Medicare Advantage: CMS Should Improve the Accuracy of Risk Score Adjustments for Diagnostic Coding Practices*, GAO-12-51 (Washington, D.C.: Jan. 12, 2012).

[29]Pub. L. No. 101-576 (1990).

collecting nearly $64 billion in fiscal year 2010, but agency responses indicated varying levels of adherence to the biennial review and reporting requirements. The survey responses indicated that for most fees, agencies (1) had not discussed fee review results in annual reports, and (2) had not reviewed the fees and were inconsistent in their ability to provide fee review documentation.

We found specific examples where a comprehensive review of user fees could lead to cost savings or enhanced revenues for the government. For example, reviewing and adjusting as needed the air passenger immigration inspection user fee to fully recover the cost of the air passenger immigration inspection activities could reduce general fund appropriations for those activities. International air passengers arriving in the United States are subject to an immigration inspection to ensure that they have legal entry and immigration documents. International air passengers pay the immigration inspection fee when they purchase their airline tickets, but the rate has not been adjusted since fiscal year 2002. In recent years, U.S. Immigration and Customs Enforcement and U.S. Customs and Border Protection, the agencies responsible for conducting inspection activities, have relied on general fund appropriations to help fund activities for which these agencies have statutory authority to fund with user fees. In fiscal year 2010, this amounted to over $120 million for the U.S. Customs and Border Protection alone. In September 2007, we recommended that the Secretary of Homeland Security report immigration inspection activity costs to ensure fees are divided between U.S. Immigration and Customs Enforcement and U.S. Customs and Border Protection according to their respective immigration inspection activity costs and to develop a legislative proposal to adjust the air passenger immigration inspection fee if it was found to not recover the costs of inspection activities. DHS agreed with our recommendations, but some of the recommendations remain unimplemented.[30] In February 2012, we suggested that Congress may wish to require the Secretary of Homeland Security to fully implement these recommendations which would serve to help to better align air passenger immigration inspection fee revenue with the costs of providing these services and achieve cost savings by reducing the reliance on general fund appropriations.

---

[30]GAO, *Federal User Fees: Key Aspects of International Air Passenger Inspection Fees Should Be Addressed Regardless of Whether Fees Are Consolidated*, GAO-07-1131 (Washington, D.C.: Sept. 24, 2007).

Similarly, we identified options for adjusting the passenger aviation security fee, a uniform fee on passengers of U.S. and foreign air carriers originating at airports in the United States. Passenger aviation security fees collected offset amounts appropriated to the Transportation Security Administration for aviation security. In recent years, several options have been considered for increasing the passenger aviation security fee. However, the fee has not been increased since it was imposed in February 2002. We suggested that Congress may wish to consider increasing the passenger security fee. Such an increase could further offset the need for appropriated funds to support civil aviation security costs from about $2 billion to $10 billion over 5 years.

- *Tax gap*: The financing of the federal government depends largely on the IRS's ability to collect federal taxes every year, which totaled $2.34 trillion in 2010. For the most part, taxpayers voluntarily report and pay their taxes on time. However the size and persistence of the tax gap— estimated in 2012 for the 2006 tax year to be a $385 billion difference between the taxes owed and taxes IRS ultimately collected for that year— highlight the need to make progress in improving compliance by those taxpayers who do not voluntarily pay what they owe. Given that tax noncompliance ranges from simple math errors to willful tax evasion, no single approach is likely to fully and cost-effectively address the tax gap. A multifaceted approach to improving compliance that includes enhancing IRS's enforcement and service capabilities can help reduce the tax gap.

One approach we have identified is the expansion of third-party information reporting, which improves taxpayer compliance and enhances IRS's enforcement capabilities. The tax gap is due predominantly to taxpayer underreporting and underpayment of taxes owed. At the same time, taxpayers are much more likely to report their income accurately when the income is also reported to IRS by a third party. By matching information received from third-party payers with what payees report on their tax returns, IRS can detect income underreporting, including the failure to file a tax return. Expanding information reporting to cover payments for services by all owners of rental real estate and to cover payments to corporations for services would improve payee compliance. The Joint Committee on Taxation estimated revenue increases of $5.9 billion over a 10-year period for just these two expansions.

Status of Actions Taken to Address the Areas Identified in 2011 Annual Report

In our 2011 annual report, we suggested a wide range of actions for the Congress and the executive branch to consider such as developing strategies to better coordinate fragmented efforts, implementing executive initiatives to improve oversight and evaluation of overlapping programs, considering enactment of legislation to facilitate revenue collection and examining opportunities to eliminate potential duplication through streamlining, collocating, or consolidating efforts or administrative services.

Our assessment of progress made as of February 10, 2012, found that 4 (or 5 percent) of the 81 areas GAO identified were addressed; 60 (or 74 percent) were partially addressed; and 17 (or 21 percent) were not addressed. Appendix I presents GAO's assessment of the overall progress made in each area. We applied the following criteria in making these overall assessments for the 81 areas. We determined that an area was:

- "addressed" if all actions needed in that area were addressed;

- "partially addressed" if at least one action needed in that area showed some progress toward implementation, but not all actions were addressed; and

- "not addressed" if none of the actions in that area were addressed.

As of February 10, 2012, the majority of 176 actions needed within the 81 areas identified by GAO have been partially addressed. Specifically, 23 (or 13 percent) were addressed;[31] 99 (or 56 percent) were partially addressed; 54 (or 31 percent) were not addressed. We applied the following criteria in making these assessments.

---

[31] In one instance, the legislative action needed required Congress to consider several options, including allowing a tax credit to expire. Thus, because Congress did not renew the provision, the action was considered addressed.

For legislative branch actions:

- "addressed," means relevant legislation is enacted and addresses all aspects of the action needed;[32]

- "partially addressed," means a relevant bill has passed a committee, the House or Senate, or relevant legislation has been enacted, but only addressed part of the action needed; and

- "not addressed," means a bill may have been introduced, but did not pass out of a committee, or no relevant legislation has been introduced.

For executive branch actions:

- "addressed," means implementation of the action needed has been completed.

- "partially addressed," means the action needed is in development; started but not yet completed; and

- "not addressed," means the administration and/or agencies have made minimal or no progress toward implementing the action needed.

In addition to the actions reported above, Congress has held a number of hearings and OMB has provided guidance to executive branch agencies on areas that we identified that could benefit from increased attention and ongoing oversight. Since the issuance of our March 2011 report, we have testified numerous times on our first annual report and on specific issues highlighted in the report.

---

[32]In situations where the action we identified as needed suggested that Congress should let a provision expire, we classified it as "addressed" if Congress permitted such expiration to happen.

GPRA Modernization Act Provides Opportunities to Address Duplication, Overlap, and Fragmentation

Many federal efforts, including those related to protecting food and agriculture, providing homeland security, and ensuring a well trained and educated workforce, transcend more than one agency, yet agencies face a range of challenges and barriers when they attempt to work collaboratively. Both Congress and the executive branch have recognized this, and in January 2011, the GPRA Modernization Act of 2010 (the Act) was enacted, updating the almost two-decades-old Government Performance and Results Act. The Act establishes a new framework aimed at taking a more crosscutting and integrated approach to focusing on results and improving government performance. Effective implementation of the Act could play an important role in clarifying desired outcomes, addressing program performance spanning multiple organizations, and facilitating future actions to reduce unnecessary duplication, overlap, and fragmentation.

The Act requires OMB to coordinate with agencies to establish outcome-oriented goals covering a limited number of crosscutting policy areas as well as goals to improve management across the federal government, and to develop a governmentwide performance plan for making progress toward achieving those goals. The performance plan is to, among other things, identify the agencies and federal activities—including spending programs, tax expenditures, and regulations—that contribute to each goal, and establish performance indicators to measure overall progress toward these goals as well as the individual contribution of the underlying agencies and federal activities. The President's budget for fiscal year 2013 includes 14 such crosscutting goals. Aspects of several of these goals—including Science, Technology, Engineering, and Math Education, Entrepreneurship and Small Businesses, Job Training, Cybersecurity, Information Technology Management, Procurement and Acquisition Management, and Real Property Management—are discussed in our 2011 or 2012 annual report. The Act also requires similar information at the agency level. Each agency is to identify the various federal organizations and activities—both within and external to the agency—that contribute to its goals, and describe how the agency is working with other agencies to achieve its goals as well as any relevant crosscutting goals. OMB officials stated that their approach to responding to this requirement will address fragmentation among federal programs.

GAO's Approach to Identifying Potential Areas for Examination

The areas identified in our annual reports are not intended to represent the full universe of duplication, overlap, or fragmentation within the federal government, but we have conducted a systematic examination across the federal government to ensure that we have identified major instances of potential duplication, overlap, and fragmentation governmentwide by the time we issue our third annual report in 2013.

Our examination involved a multiphased approach. First, to identify potential areas of overlap, we examined the major budget functions and sub-functions of the federal government as identified by OMB.[33] This was particularly helpful in identifying issue areas involving multiple government agencies. Second, our subject matter experts examined key missions and functions of federal agencies—or organizations within large agencies—using key agency documents, such as strategic plans, agency organizational charts, and mission and function documents. This further enabled us to identify areas where multiple agencies have similar goals, or where multiple organizations within federal agencies are involved in similar activities. Next, we canvassed a wide range of published sources—such as congressional hearings and reports by the Congressional Budget Office, OMB, various government audit agencies, and private think tanks—that addressed potential issues of duplication, overlap, and fragmentation. We have work under way or planned in the coming year to evaluate major instances of duplication, overlap, or fragmentation that we have not yet covered in our first two annual reports.

Identifying, preventing, and addressing unnecessary duplication, overlap, and fragmentation within the federal government is clearly challenging. These are difficult issues to address because they may require agencies and Congress to re-examine within and across various mission areas the fundamental structure, operation, funding, and performance of a number of long-standing federal programs or activities with entrenched constituencies. Implementing the Act—such as its emphasis on establishing priority outcome-oriented goals, including those covering crosscutting policy areas—could play an important role in clarifying desired outcomes, addressing program performance spanning multiple organizations, and facilitating future actions to reduce unnecessary

---

[33]The federal budget is divided into 18 broad areas (functions). Each function, in turn, is divided into basic groupings of programs, called sub-functions.

duplication, overlap, and fragmentation. Continued oversight by Congress and OMB will also be critical.

In conclusion Mr. Chairman, Ranking Member Cummings, and Members of the Committee, opportunities exist for the Congress and federal agencies to continue to address the identified actions needed in our 2011 and 2012 annual reports. Collectively, these reports show that, if the actions are implemented, the government could potentially save tens of billions of dollars annually. A number of the issues are difficult to address and implementing many of the actions identified will take time and sustained leadership. This concludes my prepared statement. I would be pleased to answer any questions you may have. Thank you.

For further information on this testimony or our February 28, 2012, reports, please contact Janet St. Laurent, Managing Director, Defense Capabilities and Management, who may be reached at (202) 512-4300, or StLaurentJ@gao.gov; and Zina Merritt, Director, Defense Capabilities and Management, who may be reached at (202) 512-4300, or MerrittZ@gao.gov. Specific questions about individual issues may be directed to the area contact listed at the end of each area summary in the reports. Contact points for our Congressional Relations and Public Affairs offices may be found on the last page of this statement.

Appendix I: Overall Progress Made in Each of the 81 Areas Identified in GAO's 2011 Annual Report

This appendix presents a summary of GAO's assessment of the overall progress made in each of the 81 areas that we identified in our March 2011 report[1] in which the Congress and the executive branch could take actions to reduce or eliminate potential duplication, overlap, and fragmentation or achieve other potential financial benefits. For each of the 34 areas related to duplication, overlap, or fragmentation that GAO identified, table 3 presents GAO's assessment of the overall progress made in implementing the actions needed in that area. For each of the 47 areas where GAO identified cost saving or revenue enhancement opportunities, table 4 presents GAO's assessment of the overall progress made in implementing the actions GAO identified.

Table 3: Overall Progress Made in Each of the GAO Identified Areas of Potential Duplication, Overlap, and Fragmentation, as of February 10, 2012

Mission	Areas identified	Assessment
Agriculture	1. Fragmented **food safety** system has caused inconsistent oversight, ineffective coordination, and inefficient use of resources	◑
Defense	2. Realigning **DOD's military medical command** structures and consolidating common functions could increase efficiency and result in projected savings ranging from $281 million to $460 million annually	◑
	3. Opportunities exist for consolidation and increased efficiencies to maximize response to **warfighter urgent needs**	◑
	4. Opportunities exist to avoid unnecessary redundancies and improve the coordination of **counter-improvised explosive device efforts**	◑
	5. Opportunities exist to avoid unnecessary redundancies and maximize the efficient use of **intelligence, surveillance,** and **reconnaissance** capabilities	◑
	6. A departmentwide acquisition strategy could reduce DOD's risk of costly duplication in purchasing **Tactical Wheeled Vehicles**	◑
	7. Improved joint oversight of DOD's **prepositioning programs** for equipment and supplies may reduce unnecessary duplication	◑
	8. **DOD's business systems** modernization: opportunities exist for optimizing business operations and systems	◑

[1]GAO, *Opportunities to Reduce Potential Duplication in Government Programs, Save Tax Dollars, and Enhance Revenue*, GAO-11-318SP (Washington, D.C.: Mar. 1, 2011).

Mission	Areas identified	Assessment
Economic development	9. The efficiency and effectiveness of fragmented **economic development programs** are unclear	◐
	10. The federal approach to **surface transportation** is fragmented, lacks clear goals, and is not accountable for results	◐
	11. Fragmented federal efforts to meet **water needs** in the **U.S.-Mexico border region** have resulted in an administrative burden, redundant activities, and an overall inefficient use of resources	○
Energy	12. Resolving conflicting requirements could more effectively achieve **federal fleet energy goals**	○
	13. Addressing duplicative federal efforts directed at increasing **domestic ethanol production** could reduce revenue losses by more than $5.7 billion annually	●
General government	14. **Enterprise architectures:** key mechanisms for identifying potential overlap and duplication	◐
	15. Consolidating **federal data** centers provides opportunity to improve government efficiency	◐
	16. Collecting improved data on **interagency contracting** to minimize duplication could help the government leverage its vast buying power	◐
	17. Periodic reviews could help identify ineffective **tax expenditures** and redundancies in related tax and spending programs, potentially reducing revenue losses by billions of dollars	○
Health	18. Opportunities exist for **DOD** and **VA** to jointly modernize their **electronic health record systems**	◐
	19. **VA** and **DOD** need to control **drug** costs and increase **joint contracting** wherever it is cost-effective	◐
	20. The Department of Health and Human Services needs an overall strategy to better integrate nationwide **public health information** systems	○
Homeland security/ Law enforcement	21. Strategic oversight mechanisms could help integrate fragmented interagency efforts to defend against **biological threats**	◐
	22. DHS oversight could help eliminate potential duplicating efforts of interagency forums in **securing** the **northern border**	○
	23. The Department of Justice plans actions to reduce overlap in **explosives investigations**, but monitoring is needed to ensure successful implementation	●
	24. **The Transportation Security Administration's (TSA) security assessments** on commercial trucking companies overlap with those of another agency, but efforts are under way to address the overlap	◐

Mission	Areas identified	Assessment
	25. DHS could streamline mechanisms for **sharing security-related information** with **public transit agencies** to help address overlapping information	◑
	26. **FEMA** needs to improve its oversight of **grants** and establish a framework for assessing capabilities to identify gaps and prioritize investments	◑
International affairs	27. Lack of information sharing could create the potential for duplication of efforts between U.S. agencies involved in **development efforts** in **Afghanistan**	◑
	28. Despite restructuring, overlapping roles and functions still exist at the Department of State's **Arms Control** and **Nonproliferation Bureaus**	●
Social services	29. Actions needed to reduce administrative overlap among **domestic food assistance** programs	○
	30. Better coordination of federal **homelessness** programs may minimize fragmentation and overlap	◑
	31. Further steps needed to improve cost-effectiveness and enhance services for **transportation-disadvantaged** persons	◑
Training, employment, and education	32. Multiple **employment** and **training** programs: providing information on collocating services and consolidating administrative structures could promote efficiencies	◑
	33. **Teacher quality**: proliferation of programs complicates federal efforts to invest dollars effectively	◑
	34. Fragmentation of **financial literacy** efforts makes coordination essential	◑

Legend:

● = Addressed, meaning all actions needed in that area were addressed.

◑= Partially addressed, meaning at least one action needed in that area showed some progress toward implementation, but not all actions were addressed.

○ = Not addressed, meaning none of the actions needed in that area were addressed.

Source: GAO analysis.

As noted above, table 4 presents GAO's assessment of the overall progress made in addressing the 47 cost-saving and revenue-enhancing areas.

Table 4: Overall Progress Made to Address GAO-Identified Cost-Saving and Revenue-Enhancing Areas, as of February 10, 2012

Mission	Areas identified	Assessment
Agriculture	35. Reducing some **farm program payments** could result in savings from $800 million over 10 years to up to $5 billion annually	◯
Defense	36. DOD should assess costs and benefits of **overseas military presence** options before committing to costly personnel realignments and construction plans, thereby possibly saving billions of dollars	◑
	37. Total compensation approach is needed to manage significant growth in **military personnel costs**	◑
	38. Employing best management practices could help DOD save money on its **weapon systems acquisition programs**	◑
	39. More efficient management could limit future costs of **DOD's spare parts** inventory	◑
	40. More comprehensive and complete cost data can help DOD improve the cost-effectiveness of **sustaining weapon systems**	◑
	41. Improved **corrosion prevention** and control practices could help DOD avoid billions in unnecessary costs over time	◑
Economic development	42. Revising the **essential air service** program could improve efficiency	◑
	43. Improved design and management of the **universal service fund** as it expands to support broadband could help avoid cost increases for consumers	◑
	44. The **Corps of Engineers** should provide Congress with project-level information on **unobligated balances**	◑
Energy	45. Improved management of federal **oil and gas resources** could result in approximately $1.8 billion over 10 years[a]	◑
General government	46. Efforts to address **governmentwide improper payments** could result in significant cost savings	◑
	47. Promoting **competition for** the over $500 billion in **federal contracts** could potentially save billions of dollars over time	◑
	48. Applying **strategic sourcing** best practices throughout the federal procurement system could saves billions of dollars annually	◑
	49. Adherence to new guidance on **award fee contracts** could improve agencies' use of award fees to produce savings	◑
	50. Agencies could realize cost savings of at least $3 billion by continued disposal of **unneeded federal real property**	◑
	51. Improved cost analyses used for making **federal facility ownership** and **leasing** decisions could save tens of millions of dollars	◑
	52. OMB's **IT Dashboard** reportedly has already resulted in $3 billion in savings and can further help identify opportunities to invest more efficiently in information technology	◑
	53. Increasing **electronic filing** of individual income **tax returns** could reduce IRS's processing costs and increase revenues by hundreds of millions of dollars	◑
	54. Using **return on investment** information to better target IRS enforcement could reduce the tax gap; for example, a 1 percent reduction would increase tax revenues by $3.8 billion[b]	◑

Mission	Areas identified	Assessment
	55. Better management of **tax debt collection** may resolve cases faster with lower IRS costs and increase debt collected	◐
	56. Broadening IRS's authority to correct **simple tax return errors** could facilitate correct tax payments and help IRS avoid costly, burdensome audits	○
	57. Enhancing **mortgage interest information** reporting could improve tax compliance	○
	58. More information on the types and uses of canceled debt could help IRS limit revenue losses of **forgiven mortgage debt**	◐
	59. Better information and outreach could help increase revenues by tens or hundreds of millions of dollars annually by addressing overstated **real estate tax deductions**	◐
	60. Revisions to content and use of **Form 1098-T** could help IRS enforce higher education requirements and increase revenues	◐
	61. Many options could improve the tax compliance of **sole proprietors** and begin to reduce their $68 billion portion of the tax gap	○
	62. IRS could find additional **businesses not filing tax returns** by using third-party data, which show such businesses have billions of dollars in sales	◐
	63. Congress and IRS can help **S corporations** and their shareholders be more tax compliant, potentially increasing tax revenues by hundreds of millions of dollars each year	◐
	64. IRS needs an agencywide approach for addressing tax evasion among the at least 1 million **networks of businesses** and related entities	◐
	65. Opportunities exist to improve the targeting of the $6 billion **research tax credit** and reduce forgone revenue	○
	66. Converting the **new markets tax credit** to a grant program may increase program efficiency and significantly reduce the $3.8 billion 5-year revenue cost of the program	○
	67. Limiting the tax-exempt status of certain **governmental bonds** could yield revenue	○
	68. Adjusting **civil tax penalties** for inflation potentially could increase revenues by tens of millions of dollars per year, not counting any revenues that may result from maintaining the penalties' deterrent effect	◐
	69. IRS may be able to systematically identify **nonresident aliens** reporting unallowed tax deductions or credits	●
	70. Tracking **undisbursed balances** in **expired grant accounts** could facilitate the reallocation of scarce resources or the return of funding to the Treasury	○
Health	71. Preventing billions in **Medicaid improper payments** requires sustained attention and action by CMS	◐
	72. Federal oversight over **Medicaid supplemental payments** needs improvement, which could lead to substantial cost savings	○
	73. Better targeting of **Medicare's** claims review could reduce **improper payments**	◐
	74. Potential savings in **Medicare's payment** for **health care**	◐

Mission	Areas identified	Assessment
Homeland security/ Law enforcement	75. **DHS's management of acquisitions** could be strengthened to reduce cost overruns and schedule and performance shortfalls	◑
	76. Improvements in **managing research and development** could help reduce inefficiencies and costs for homeland security	◑
	77. Validation of **TSA's behavior-based screening program** is needed to justify funding or expansion	◑
	78. More efficient **baggage screening systems** could result in about $470 million in reduced TSA personnel costs over the next 5 years	◑
	79. Clarifying availability of certain **customs fee collections** could produce a one-time savings of $640 million	◑
Income security	80. **Social Security** needs data on pensions from noncovered earnings to better enforce **offsets** and ensure benefit fairness, estimated to result in $2.4-$2.9 billion savings over 10 years	○
International affairs	81. Congress could pursue several options to improve collection of **antidumping** and **countervailing duties.**	○

Legend:

● = Addressed, meaning all actions needed in that area were addressed.

◑= Partially addressed, meaning at least one action needed in that area showed some progress toward implementation, but not all actions were addressed.

○ = Not addressed, meaning none of the actions needed in that area were addressed.

Source: GAO analysis.

[a]The Department of the Interior, Bureau of Land Management, updated the anticipated revenues from $1.75 billion to $1.8 billion in its fiscal year 2012 budget justification.

[b]The net tax gap was updated in 2012 and estimated to be $385 billion for the 2006 tax year. Thus, a 1 percent reduction would increase tax revenues by $3.8 billion.

GAO's Mission	The Government Accountability Office, the audit, evaluation, and investigative arm of Congress, exists to support Congress in meeting its constitutional responsibilities and to help improve the performance and accountability of the federal government for the American people. GAO examines the use of public funds; evaluates federal programs and policies; and provides analyses, recommendations, and other assistance to help Congress make informed oversight, policy, and funding decisions. GAO's commitment to good government is reflected in its core values of accountability, integrity, and reliability.
Obtaining Copies of GAO Reports and Testimony	The fastest and easiest way to obtain copies of GAO documents at no cost is through GAO's website (www.gao.gov). Each weekday afternoon, GAO posts on its website newly released reports, testimony, and correspondence. To have GAO e-mail you a list of newly posted products, go to www.gao.gov and select "E-mail Updates."
Order by Phone	The price of each GAO publication reflects GAO's actual cost of production and distribution and depends on the number of pages in the publication and whether the publication is printed in color or black and white. Pricing and ordering information is posted on GAO's website, http://www.gao.gov/ordering.htm. Place orders by calling (202) 512-6000, toll free (866) 801-7077, or TDD (202) 512-2537. Orders may be paid for using American Express, Discover Card, MasterCard, Visa, check, or money order. Call for additional information.
Connect with GAO	Connect with GAO on Facebook, Flickr, Twitter, and YouTube. Subscribe to our RSS Feeds or E-mail Updates. Listen to our Podcasts. Visit GAO on the web at www.gao.gov.
To Report Fraud, Waste, and Abuse in Federal Programs	Contact: Website: www.gao.gov/fraudnet/fraudnet.htm E-mail: fraudnet@gao.gov Automated answering system: (800) 424-5454 or (202) 512-7470
Congressional Relations	Katherine Siggerud, Managing Director, siggerudk@gao.gov, (202) 512-4400, U.S. Government Accountability Office, 441 G Street NW, Room 7125, Washington, DC 20548
Public Affairs	Chuck Young, Managing Director, youngc1@gao.gov, (202) 512-4800 U.S. Government Accountability Office, 441 G Street NW, Room 7149 Washington, DC 20548

Please Print on Recycled Paper.

www.ingramcontent.com/pod-product-compliance
Lightning Source LLC
Chambersburg PA
CBHW080915290526
45795CB00007BA/2528